The cross-country race

Story by Jenny Giles

Illustrated by Trish Hill

Mrs. Hill said to her class, "I'm going to take you for a long run, every day. Then you will be ready for our cross-country race. Come on, let's warm up before we start."

3

up the hill →

behind the trees →

over the grass

START   FINISH

Every day the children ran
over the grass,
up the hill,
behind the trees,
by the fence,
around the fort,
past the school,

ac

by the fence →

around the fort

across the playground
and all the way back
to the start.

past the school

Hilltop School

e playground

Tim and Michael and Anna
were all good runners,
but Tim was the best.

Tim's friend Michael said,
"Tim will come in first on race day."

"Yes," said Anna. "Tim will win."

On the day of the cross-country race
everyone came to see
the children run.

"On your mark . . . get set . . .
GO!" said Mr. James
to class after class.

Off went Tim's class . . .
over the grass, up the hill
and behind the trees.

Tim, Anna and Michael
ran very fast.
Tim wanted to win.
He **was** winning.

But then Michael fell over.
He did not get up.
Tim looked back
and saw Michael on the ground.
He went to help him.

The class ran on . . .
and Anna won the race.

The two boys walked back slowly.
Mr. James went to meet them.
"Let's have a look at your leg,
Michael," he said.

Michael said to Mr. James,
"Tim stopped to help me,
and he was going to **win**!"

"Tim is a very
good friend,"
said Mr. James.
"Let's all
give him
a big cheer!"
And everyone
did.